10|98

Herons

*written and photographed
by Frank Staub*

 Lerner Publications Company • Minneapolis, Minnesota

For Mom, my favorite bird-watcher

Photograph on page 40 reproduced through the courtesy of Everglades National Park.

Thanks to our series consultant, Sharyn Fenwick, elementary science/math specialist. Mrs. Fenwick was the winner of the National Science Teachers Association 1991 Distinguished Teaching Award. She also was the recipient of the Presidential Award for Excellence in Math and Science Teaching, representing the state of Minnesota at the elementary level in 1992. And special thanks to our young helper, Danielle Wold.

Early Bird Nature Books were conceptualized by Ruth Berman and designed by Steve Foley. Series editor is Joelle Goldman.

Library of Congress Cataloging-in-Publication Data

Staub, Frank J.
    Herons / written and photographed by Frank Staub.
      p. cm. – (Early bird nature books)
    Includes index.
    Summary: Describes the physical characteristics and
  behavior of various species of herons, as well as their mating
  habits and hunting methods.
    ISBN 0-8225-3017-1 (alk. paper)
    1. Herons—Juvenile literature. [1. Herons.] I. Title.
II. Series.
QL696.C52S87 1997
598.3'4—DC20   96-36609

Manufactured in the United States of America
1 2 3 4 5 6 – SP – 02 01 00 99 98 97

Contents

A tricolored heron perches on a tree branch.

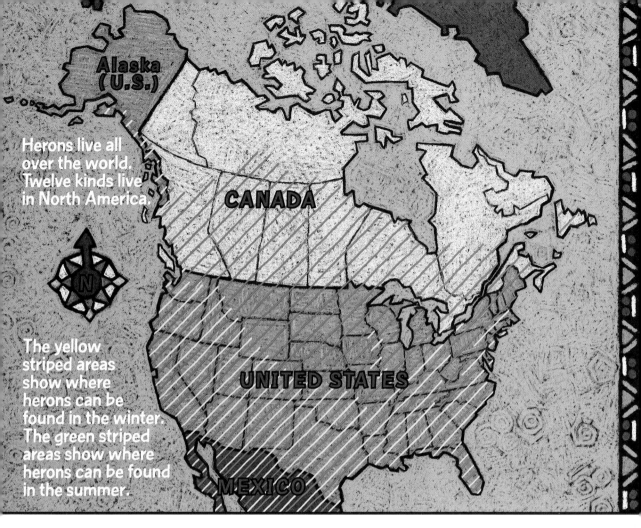

Alaska (U.S.)

Herons live all over the world. Twelve kinds live in North America.

N

The yellow striped areas show where herons can be found in the winter. The green striped areas show where herons can be found in the summer.

CANADA

UNITED STATES

MEXICO

Be a Word Detective

Can you find these words as you read about the heron's life? Be a detective and try to figure out what they mean. You can turn to the glossary on page 47 for help.

down	incubate	preen
display	plumes	roost
extinct	powder down	wetlands
heronry		

Chapter 1

A heron lands in the water. Why do herons have long legs?

The Quiet Hunter

 It's a quiet morning on the pond. There's no wind, and the water is calm. Then a large bird flies in. It lands in the shallow water near the shore. It stands without moving.

Long skinny legs hold its body high so it doesn't get wet. And a long neck makes the bird as tall as you. The bird is a great blue heron (HEH-run).

The great blue heron is the largest heron in North America. It stands 4 feet tall.

The tall bird stares down into the water. It moves its head to the left, then to the right. Suddenly, the heron's pointy beak shoots down like a spear. And the quiet hunter comes up with a wiggling meal.

This great blue heron can catch fish without bending its legs. If the heron had to bend its legs, the fish might know it was coming.

The yellow-crowned night heron has a thicker body, shorter neck, and shorter legs than most other herons.

There are about 60 species, or kinds, of herons. Some are large, and some are small. Some are white, and some have red, blue, green, gray, or black feathers. But every heron has long legs, a long neck, and a long pointed bill, or beak.

9

Twelve members of the heron family live in North America. Six have the word *heron* in their names. Four others are called egrets (EE-grets). And two species are called bitterns. Bitterns spend their time hidden among plants. But most herons stay out in the open.

A least bittern perches on marsh grasses. Least bitterns are only about 1 foot long. They're very shy.

Left: *A little blue heron stands out in the open.*

Below: *The reddish egret runs and hops when it hunts for food. It looks like it is dancing.*

A great blue heron holds its neck in an S shape.
The great blue heron is the largest heron in
North America.

Herons look much like other waterbirds, such as storks and cranes. All these birds have long legs and long necks. When storks and cranes fly, they stick their necks out straight. But a flying heron usually bends its neck into an S shape. And when a heron walks or stands, it usually rests its neck in a graceful curve.

When a heron wants to fly, it spreads its wings. Then it moves its wings downward. The wings push against the air, and the heron takes off. As it flies, its legs dangle out behind its body.

A snowy egret glides through the air. The snowy egret is the only heron in North America that has yellow feet.

When a flying heron is ready to land, it needs to slow down. A fast, hard landing might break its skinny legs. So herons need good brakes. A bird's brakes are its wings. Just before it lands, a heron pushes air forward with its wings. This slows it down.

Wide wings slow a bird down more than narrow wings do. Like all herons, the snowy egret has wide wings so it can land slowly and easily.

14

A heron's body is built for living in wetlands. Wetlands are the places where land and water meet. They are found along the edges of streams, rivers, lakes, and oceans.

A great egret perches on a log in a swamp. Swamps, bogs, and marshes are all wetlands.

Herons don't float on the water like ducks do. Herons wade. Walking in slippery mud and squishy plants can be tricky. So herons have long toes to help them balance. And their long legs hold their bodies above the water.

A tricolored heron walks in slippery mud.

A green heron wraps its long toes around a branch.

Herons live in most of North America. But they don't like cold weather. Some herons live in places that have cold winters. These herons fly to warmer places when the weather gets bad. And you won't find herons in the far north, even in the summer.

Chapter 2

On this great blue heron's sides, you can see white down feathers. What are down feathers?

Keeping Clean and Dry

Like all other birds, herons have feathers. Feathers protect a bird's skin. They also hold air. The air in their feathers keeps birds warm. Down feathers are special feathers that are little and wispy. They grow under the big feathers, next to a bird's skin.

Wet feathers don't hold air. So a wet bird is a cold bird. And wet feathers are heavier than dry feathers. Wet feathers may make a bird too heavy to fly.

A great blue heron stands in deep water. Its long legs help to keep its feathers dry.

Herons must be extra careful to keep their feathers dry. After all, they're near water a lot. So herons preen to make their feathers waterproof. When herons preen, they use their bills to spread powder down on their feathers. Powder down is a kind of down that grows on

A great egret preens. The great egret is the most common heron in North America.

Preening helps this little blue heron clean fish slime and dirt from its feathers.

herons. When powder down is touched, it crumbles into powder.

Powder down is waterproof. It keeps water out of a heron's feathers. Raindrops and splashes just roll off.

Preening also keeps the heron's feathers clean. Dirt sticks to the powder down. Then the heron uses its toes to comb dirty powder out of its feathers.

Chapter 3

This great egret is swallowing a water snake whole. What other animals do herons like to eat?

Nabbing Meals

Wetlands are full of life. So they're good places for herons to find food. Herons eat fish, frogs, snakes, bugs, and other little animals. Some herons hunt by standing still and waiting for a meal to come near. But most herons walk while they hunt. Herons with very long legs can hunt in deep water. Herons with shorter legs stay in shallow water.

A little blue heron has caught a crayfish in its long pointy bill.

Some herons shuffle their feet as they hunt. This scares underwater animals. The animals move to get out of the heron's way. A moving animal is easier to spot than an animal that is still. So shuffling helps herons catch food.

Other herons fly close to the water. As they fly, they dip their bills down to nab fish.

A tricolored heron flies just above the water's surface to catch fish.

Cattle egrets catch insects and other little animals stirred up by a walking cow.

Cattle egrets let cattle scare up their meals. When cattle walk, insects jump and fly to get out of the way. Cattle egrets walk with the moving cattle. They snatch up the insects as they move.

Chapter 4

Cattle egrets are usually all white. But one of these cattle egrets has orange feathers on its head and chest. What do the colored feathers mean?

"Birds of a Feather"?

When a heron is ready to have chicks, its bill, face, legs, or feet may change color. Some herons may grow brightly colored feathers. Some grow big feathers called plumes. Plumes may make enemies think herons look big and dangerous. Plumes may also make herons look better to other herons.

Great egrets grow plumes that may be over 1 foot long. When great egrets are ready to nest, green appears near their eyes.

During its display, a great egret sticks its plumes out.

Displays are the way herons talk to each other. During a display, a heron may fluff up its plumes and make them stick out. It may

A yellow-crowned night heron displays while its mate preens.

stretch its neck, move its head, snap its bill, or shake a twig. It may fly in a circle. Or it may make a hoarse, raspy, croaking sound.

Male and female herons often display to each other. Their displays say that they want to be together. Herons also display to scare other herons away. Or they may display just to say "hi."

Plumes and displays also help herons to tell each other apart. This is important because many herons live together. They live in groups called heronries. A heronry is a place where herons roost, or rest, in the trees. It's also a place where herons make nests. Some heronries have hundreds of nests. Some have just a few.

This heronry contains just a few great egrets.

Heronries may be a mile or more away from the place where the birds go to eat.

Did you ever hear someone say, "Birds of a feather flock together"? This means that birds of the same species usually live together. Groups of birds are called flocks. A flock usually has just one species of bird. But herons are different from many other birds. A heronry may contain more than one heron species. Even birds who aren't herons may roost and nest in a heronry.

Chapter 5

Two yellow-crowned night herons perch on their nest. Which heron builds the nest—the female or the male?

Nesting and Family Life

 Like most birds, herons make nests in the spring. They usually build their nests in trees. There herons are safe from most of their enemies. Each pair of herons builds a nest.

32

The male brings sticks and twigs, and the female puts them into place.

A flying egret carries nesting material to his mate. She is standing at the right, calling out. These egrets are nesting on platforms people built for them.

Small herons build small nests, and big herons build big nests. A big heron nest may be up to 3 feet across. Heron nests look shaky, as if they might blow away in the wind. But a heron nest is strong. Herons may use it again, year after year.

A great blue heron stands on its shaky-looking nest.

A great egret lays light blue eggs. Other heron species lay white or light green eggs.

Each spring, a female heron lays 3 to 6 eggs. The female and male take turns sitting on the eggs. This is called incubation. Incubation keeps the eggs from getting too warm during the day or too cool at night.

Herons incubate their eggs for 3 to 4 weeks. Then the eggs hatch. The new chicks are helpless. They can see, but they can't fly. They can't even walk. They are covered with fluffy down. Their regular feathers grow in later.

Young great egret chicks are covered with down.

A great egret chick grabs its parent's bill to make the parent throw up food.

Both parents feed the chicks. When a parent returns from a hunting trip, a chick grabs its bill. This makes the parent throw up food. The chicks gobble the food up quickly. As the chicks get older, they can eat food that the parents haven't swallowed first.

These young egrets have grown adult feathers. But they still ask for food from their parents.

During some years, there is little food for herons to eat. Then many chicks don't get enough to eat, and they die. Some chicks get blown out of nests during storms. And some are snatched up by owls, hawks, or crows.

After a month or two, the chicks have grown enough to leave the nest. Then they learn to fly. But their parents still help them find food. When they are two or three months old, the young herons can hunt on their own.

This young reddish egret is colored differently than an adult. Can you find pictures of adult reddish egrets in this book?

Chapter 6

During the late 1800s, many women liked to wear feathers in their hats. What kind of feathers were their favorite?

When Feathers Were the Fashion

 In the late 1800s, women liked to wear feathers on their hats. Their favorite feathers were the long plumes of egrets. An ounce of plumes cost more than an ounce of gold.

Plumes grow during the nesting season. So egrets were often killed while they were incubating eggs or raising chicks. Many chicks died because hunters shot their parents.

It was easy for plume hunters to kill great egrets who were sitting on their nests.

By 1900, many herons had been killed. There were few herons left alive. If a species of animal is completely killed off, it is extinct. But before any herons became extinct, many people

This tricolored heron lives in Everglades National Park. Animals who live in national parks are protected from hunters.

got angry. They got thousands of women to stop buying hats with feathers. The government made laws to protect herons.

Now there are many herons. So if you see a bird with long skinny legs, a long curved neck, and a long pointy bill, it's probably a heron.

The pointed bill and the curved neck of this reddish egret tell you it's in the heron family.

On Sharing a Book

As you know, adults greatly influence a child's attitude toward reading. When a child sees you read, or when you share a book with a child, you're sending a message that reading is important. Show the child that reading a book together is important to you. Find a comfortable, quiet place. Turn off the television and limit other distractions such as telephone calls.

Be prepared to start slowly. Take turns reading parts of this book. Stop and talk about what you're reading. Talk about the photographs. You may find that much of the shared time is spent discussing just a few pages. This discussion time is valuable for both of you, so don't move through the book too quickly. If the child begins to lose interest, stop reading. Continue sharing the book at another time. When you do pick up the book again, be sure to revisit the parts you have already read. Most importantly, enjoy the book!

Be a Vocabulary Detective

You will find a word list on page 5. Words selected for this list are important to the understanding of the topic of this book. Encourage the child to be a word detective and search for the words as you read the book together. Talk about what the words mean and how they are used in the sentence. Do any of these words have more than one meaning? You will find these words defined in a glossary on page 46.

What about Questions?

Use questions to make sure the child understands the information in this book. Here are some suggestions:

> What did this paragraph tell us? What does this picture show? What do you think we'll learn about next? Could a heron live in your neighborhood? Why/Why not? Where do herons build their nests? How does a heron use its long neck? How is a heronry like your home and how is it different? (Are there different species in your home like there are in a heronry?) What do you think it's like being a heron? What if there were no herons? What is your favorite part of the book? Why?

If the child has questions, don't hesitate to respond with questions of your own such as: What do *you* think? Why? What is it that you don't know? If the child can't remember certain facts, turn to the index.

Introducing the Index

The index is an important learning tool. It helps readers get information quickly without searching throughout the whole book. Turn to the index on page 48. Choose an entry such as *preening* and ask the child to use the index to find out how herons preen. Repeat this exercise with as many entries as you like. Ask the child to point out the differences between an index and a glossary. (The index helps readers find information quickly, while the glossary tells readers what words mean.)

All the World in Metric

Although our monetary system is in metric units (based on multiples of 10), the United States is one of the few countries in the world that does not use the metric system of measurement. Here are some conversion activities you and the child can do using a calculator:

WHEN YOU KNOW:	MULTIPLY BY:	TO FIND:
miles	1.609	kilometers
feet	0.3048	meters
inches	2.54	centimeters
gallons	3.787	liters
pounds	0.454	kilograms

Activities

Make up a story about herons. Be sure information from this book is included. Then illustrate the story.

Watch the birds in your neighborhood as they fly, look for food, or talk to each other. How are they similar to herons? How are they different?

Put on your rain boots and walk around in the mud. Would it be easier to walk in the mud if you had long toes and skinny legs like a heron?

Collect some dead sticks and twigs from the ground. Weave sticks together into a nest shape. Can you build a nest that doesn't fall apart when you pick it up? It's very hard for people to build nests, but herons do it well. How do you think herons build nests that are so strong?

Glossary

down—fine, soft feathers that cover baby birds and that are under the big feathers of adult birds

displays—a position or action performed by an animal to communicate with other animals

extinct—plants or animals that no longer exist

heronry—a place where herons gather and have their young

incubate—when a bird sits on its eggs

plumes—large, showy feathers

powder down—a special kind of down that crumbles into powder

preen—to smooth feathers with a beak

roost—when birds are in the place where they will spend the night

wetlands—land areas with a lot of moisture, like swamps, bogs, or marshes

Index

Pages listed in **bold** type refer to photographs.